How to Draw Funny People

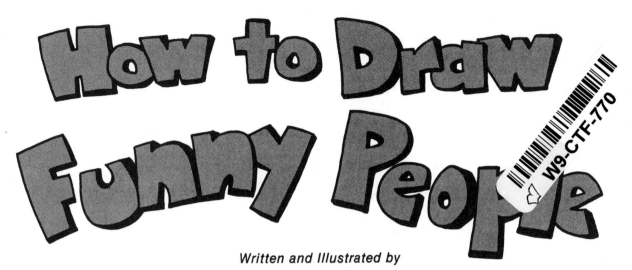

Written and Illustrated by
Bob McKay

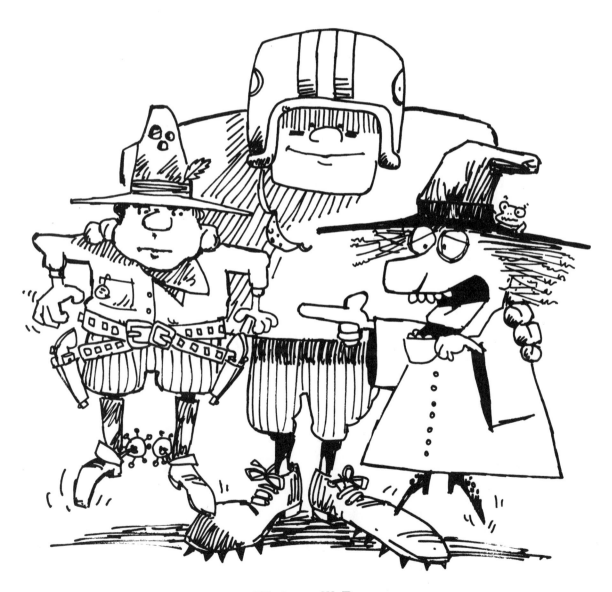

Watermill Press

Copyright © by Troll Communications L.L.C.
Published by Watermill Press, an imprint and registered trademark
of Troll Communications L.L.C.
10 9 8 7 6 5 4 3

Materials

The only materials you'll need to do the first two steps of these drawings are a medium or soft pencil. A fine-to-medium point black felt-tip marker pen can be used to do the line work of the final drawing. (Marker pens are easier to work with than a pen and ink.) To do the shading, use a No. 3 gray and a No. 6 gray wide-tip marker pen. They can be purchased at any art supply store. The marker pens work well because you can cover a large area very fast, and the ink dries as quickly as you put it on the paper. Any white paper can be used, but it should be at least 8½″ × 11″. A pad of tracing paper will be helpful, too. You'll also need an eraser. But if you really think about what you do before you start to draw, you won't need that eraser often.

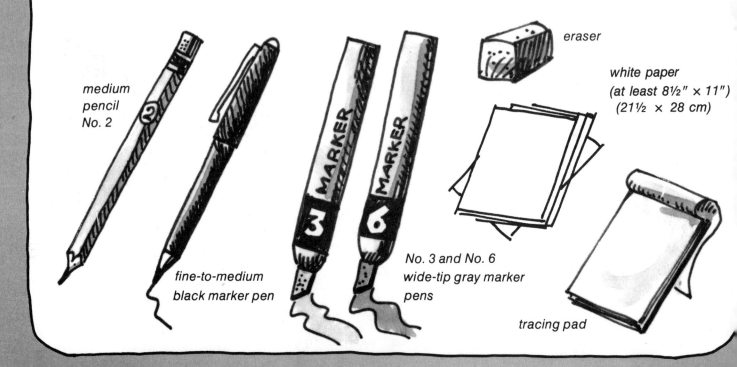

medium
pencil
No. 2

fine-to-medium
black marker pen

No. 3 and No. 6
wide-tip gray marker
pens

eraser

white paper
(at least 8½″ × 11″)
(21½ × 28 cm)

tracing pad

Basic Shapes

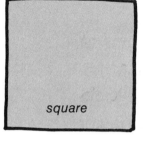
square

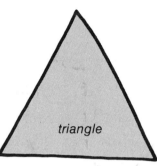
triangle

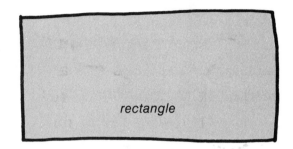
rectangle

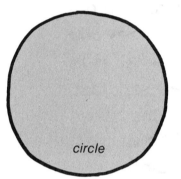
circle

These are the basic shapes that are always used when drawing people, animals, and things. As you draw the funny people in this book, you will see that these shapes are used to start the drawings. They will give you the general size and shape of the person.

Do the first two steps lightly in pencil. Then connect the shapes and add detail with black marker pen. Finally, using gray marker pen, add the shading and style that make it your drawing.

Try tracing some of the drawings in this book first. It will help you get a good idea of the shapes, sizes, and proportions.

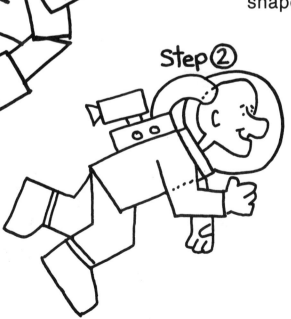
Step ①

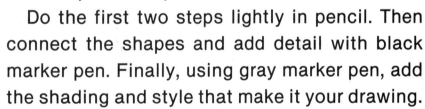
Step ②

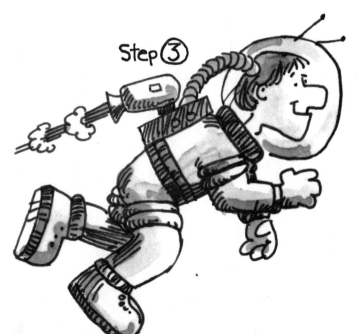
Step ③

Expressions

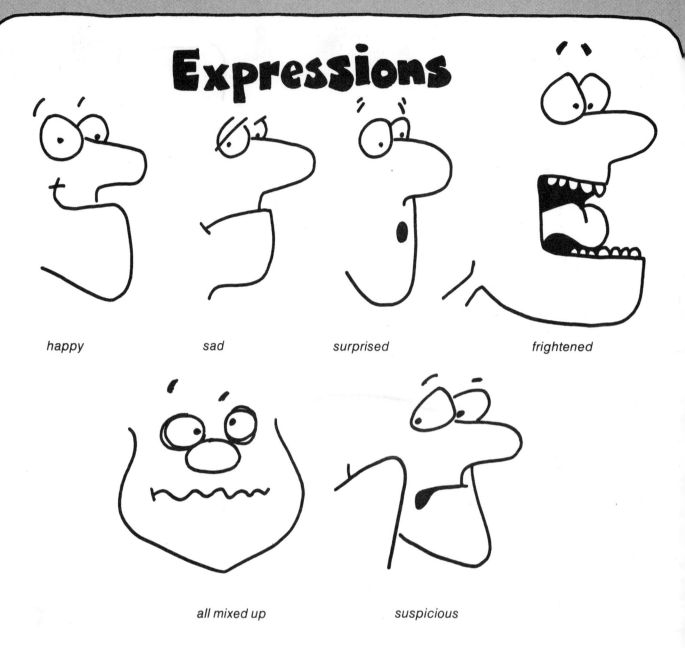

happy   sad   surprised   frightened

all mixed up   suspicious

Look at yourself in the mirror and make all of these expressions. See what happens to your eyes, eyebrows, and mouth.

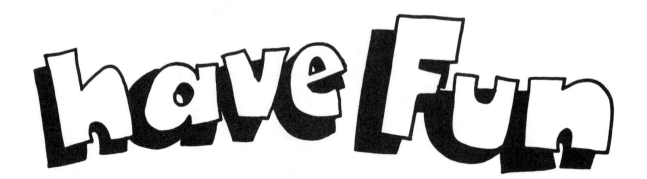

The fish that got away.

(always exaggerate when drawing funny people)

1   Draw big feet on little people. Draw little feet on big people.
2   A big mouth should be drawn really big.
3   Thin legs should be really skinny with knobby knees.
4   A big nose should be really big.

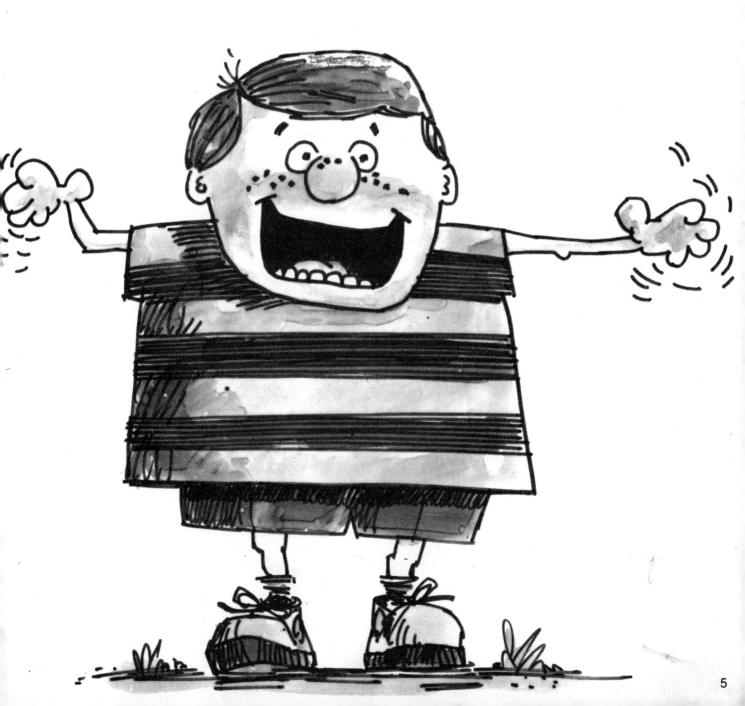

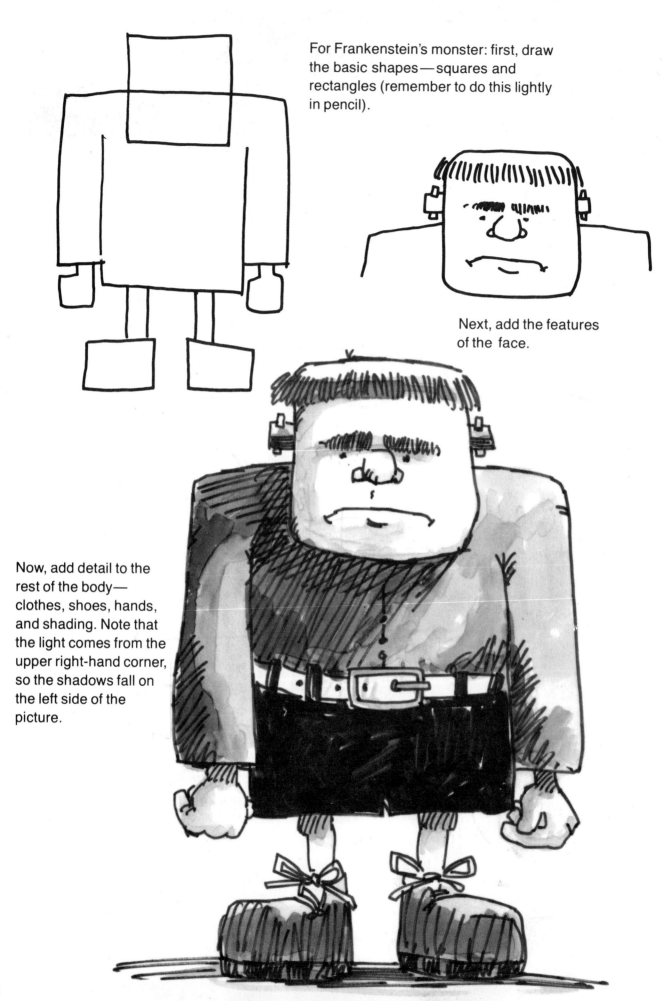

For Frankenstein's monster: first, draw the basic shapes—squares and rectangles (remember to do this lightly in pencil).

Next, add the features of the face.

Now, add detail to the rest of the body— clothes, shoes, hands, and shading. Note that the light comes from the upper right-hand corner, so the shadows fall on the left side of the picture.

SPACE RANGER

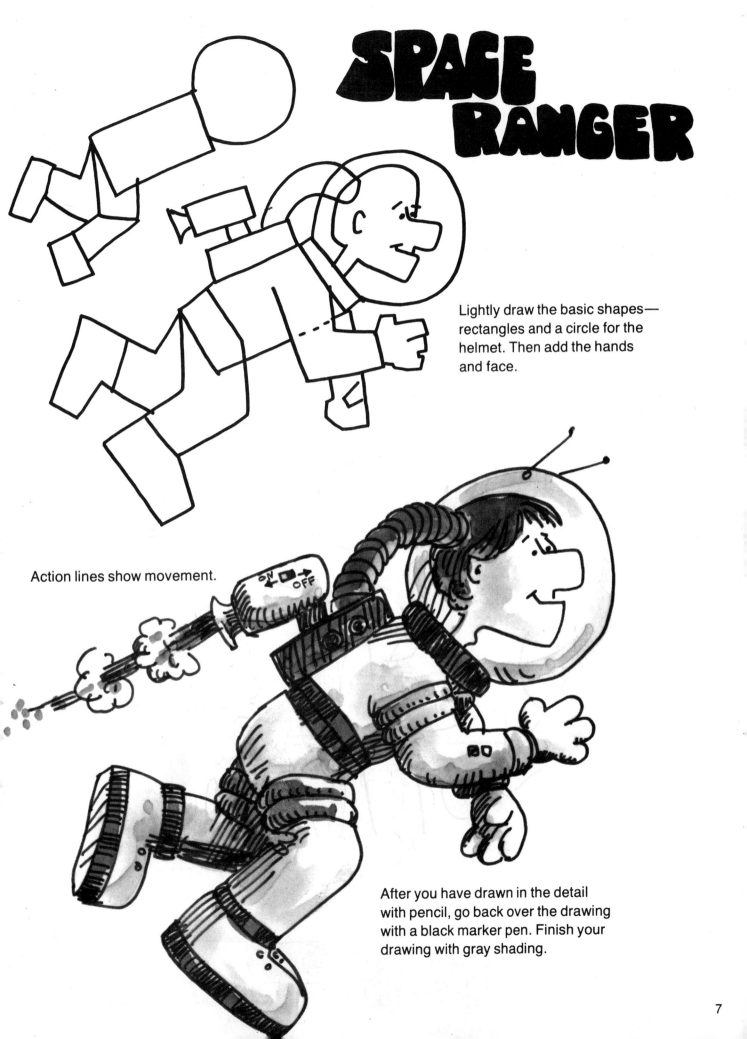

Lightly draw the basic shapes—rectangles and a circle for the helmet. Then add the hands and face.

Action lines show movement.

After you have drawn in the detail with pencil, go back over the drawing with a black marker pen. Finish your drawing with gray shading.

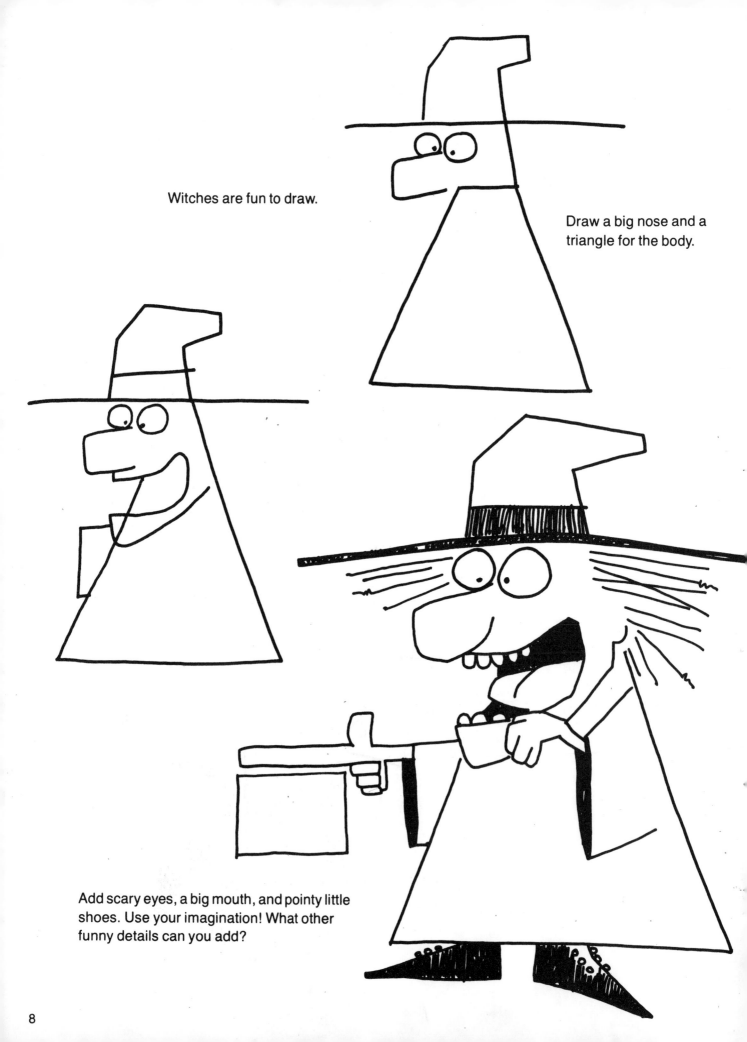

Witches are fun to draw.

Draw a big nose and a triangle for the body.

Add scary eyes, a big mouth, and pointy little shoes. Use your imagination! What other funny details can you add?

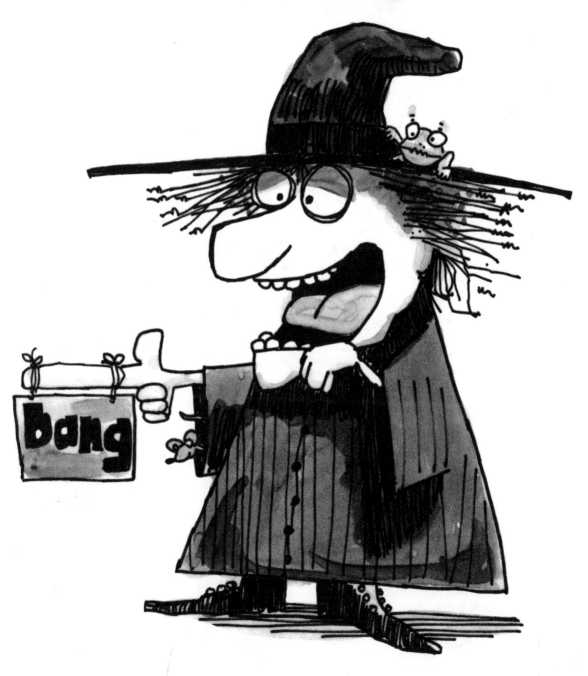

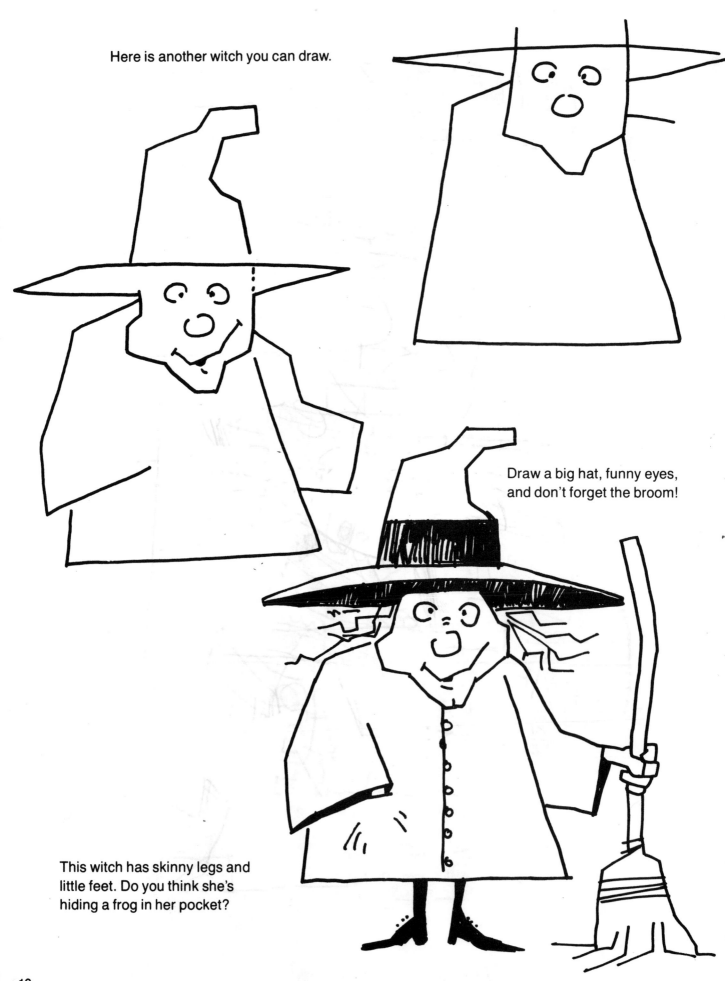

Here is another witch you can draw.

Draw a big hat, funny eyes, and don't forget the broom!

This witch has skinny legs and little feet. Do you think she's hiding a frog in her pocket?

ABRACADABRA

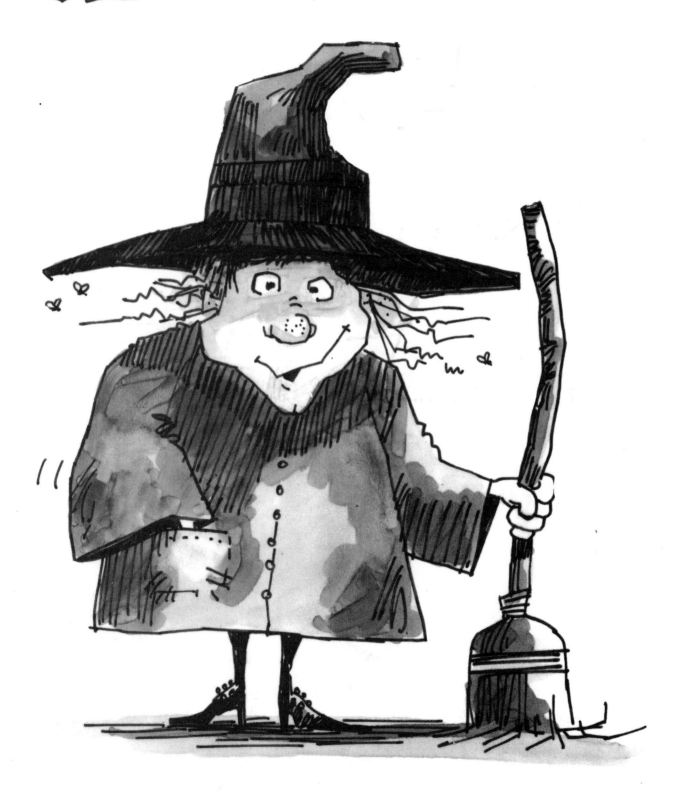

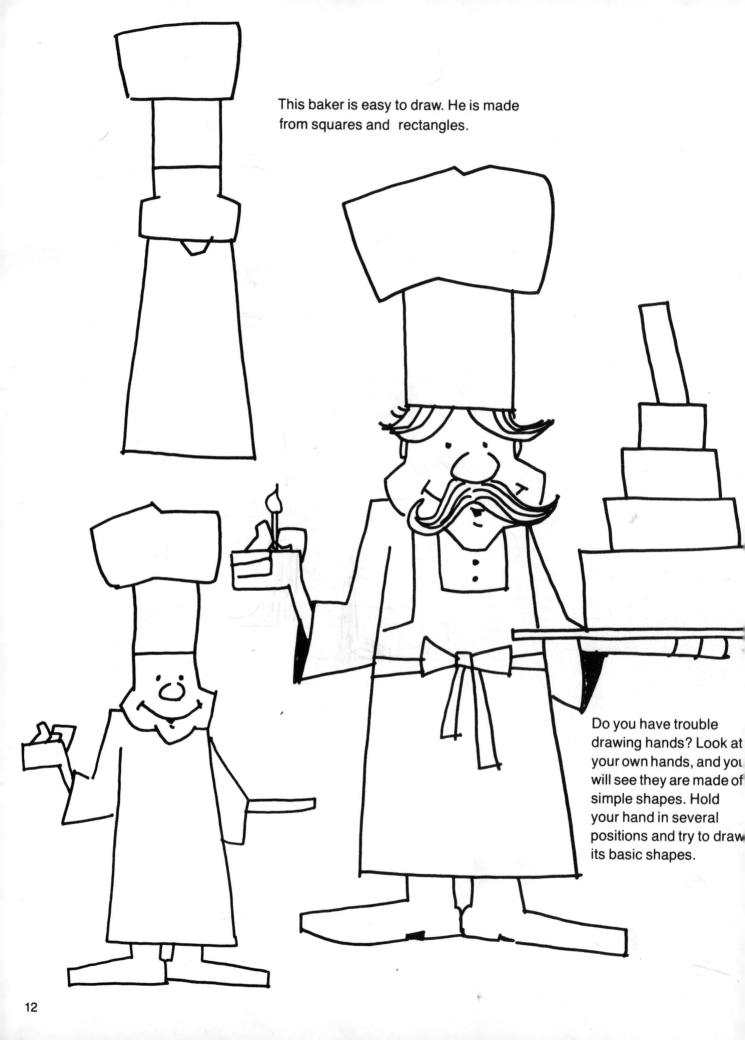

This baker is easy to draw. He is made from squares and rectangles.

Do you have trouble drawing hands? Look at your own hands, and you will see they are made of simple shapes. Hold your hand in several positions and try to draw its basic shapes.

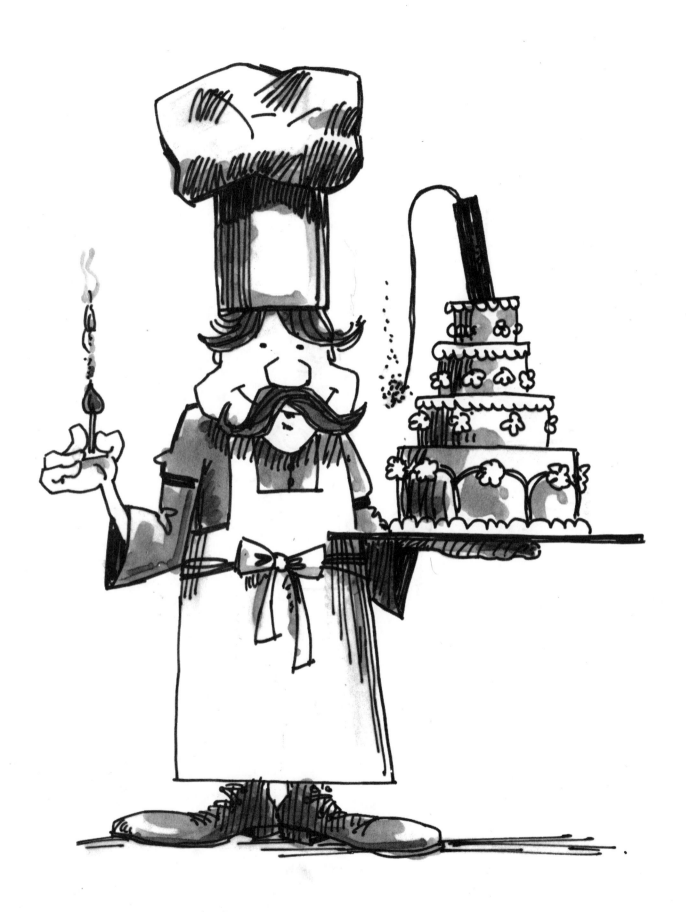

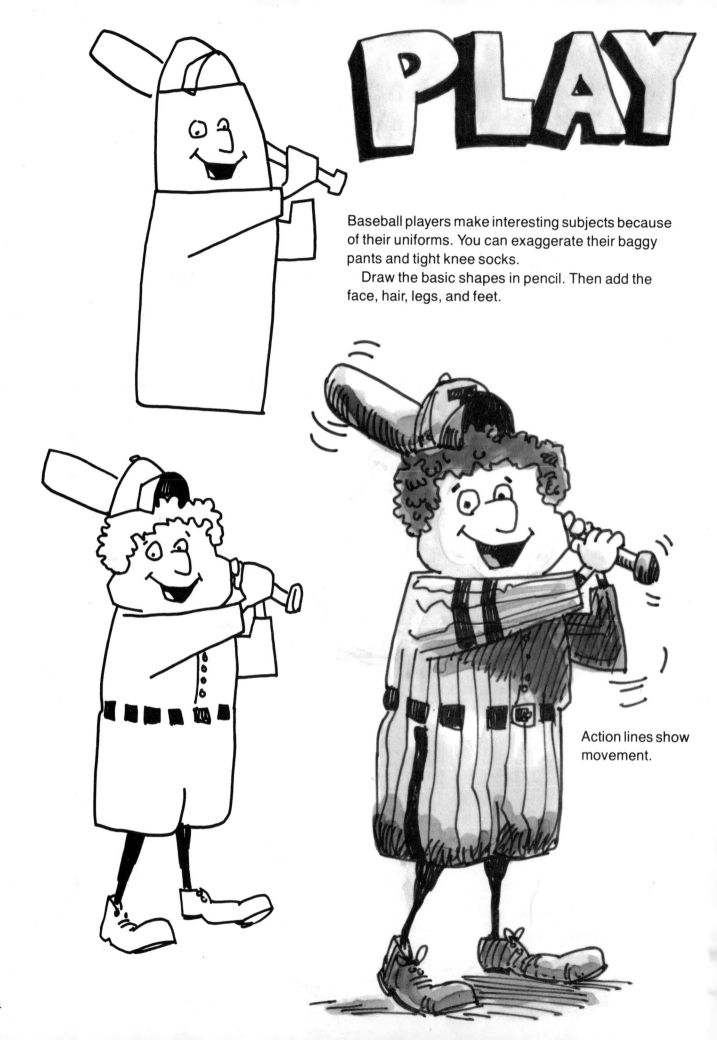

PLAY

Baseball players make interesting subjects because of their uniforms. You can exaggerate their baggy pants and tight knee socks.

Draw the basic shapes in pencil. Then add the face, hair, legs, and feet.

Action lines show movement.

BALL

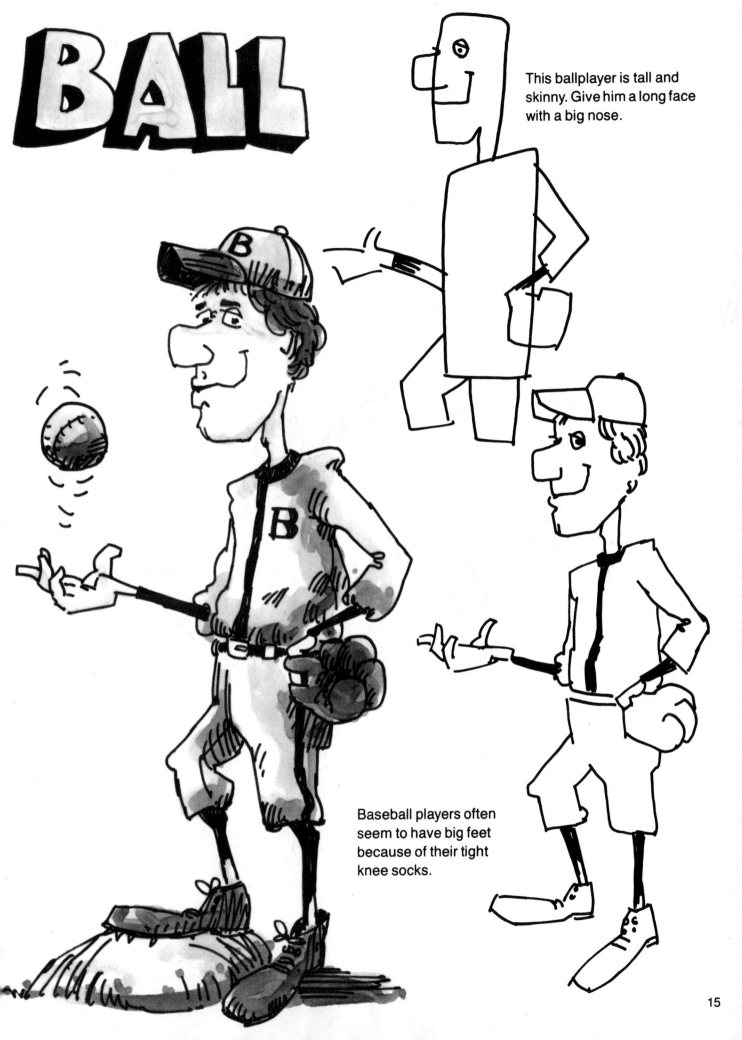

This ballplayer is tall and skinny. Give him a long face with a big nose.

Baseball players often seem to have big feet because of their tight knee socks.

15

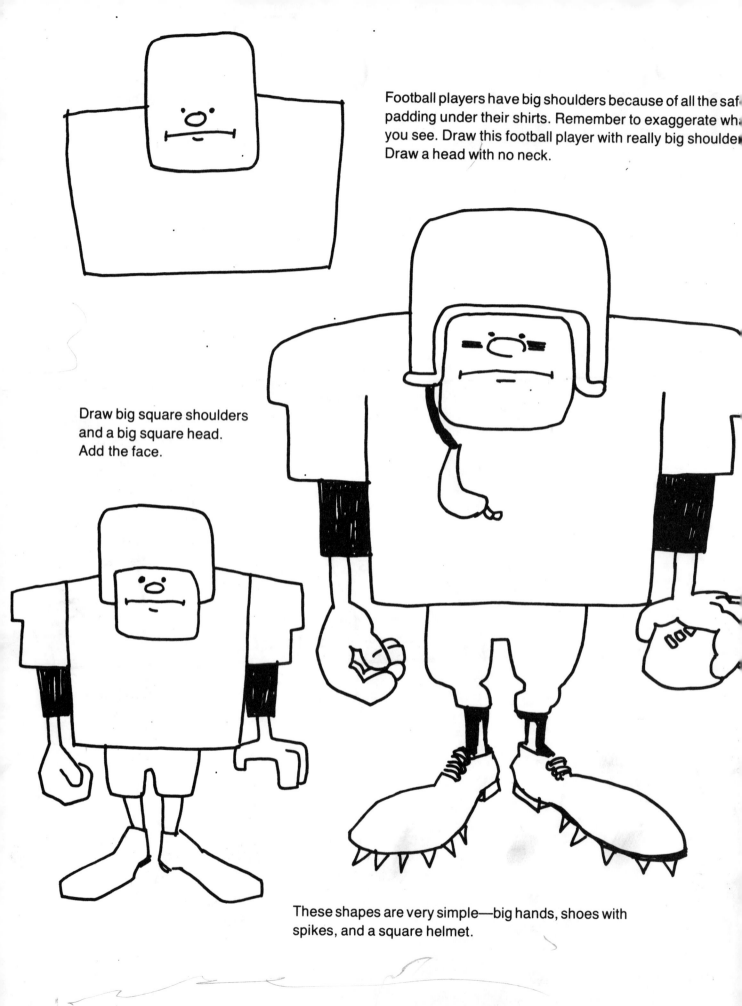

Football players have big shoulders because of all the safe
padding under their shirts. Remember to exaggerate wha
you see. Draw this football player with really big shoulde
Draw a head with no neck.

Draw big square shoulders
and a big square head.
Add the face.

These shapes are very simple—big hands, shoes with
spikes, and a square helmet.

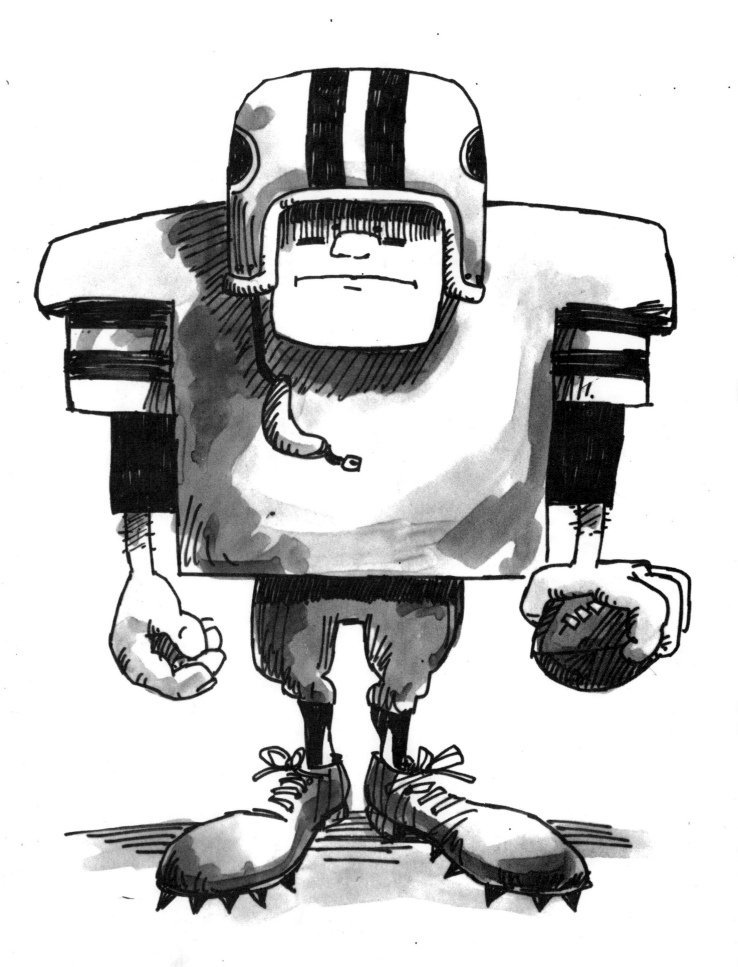

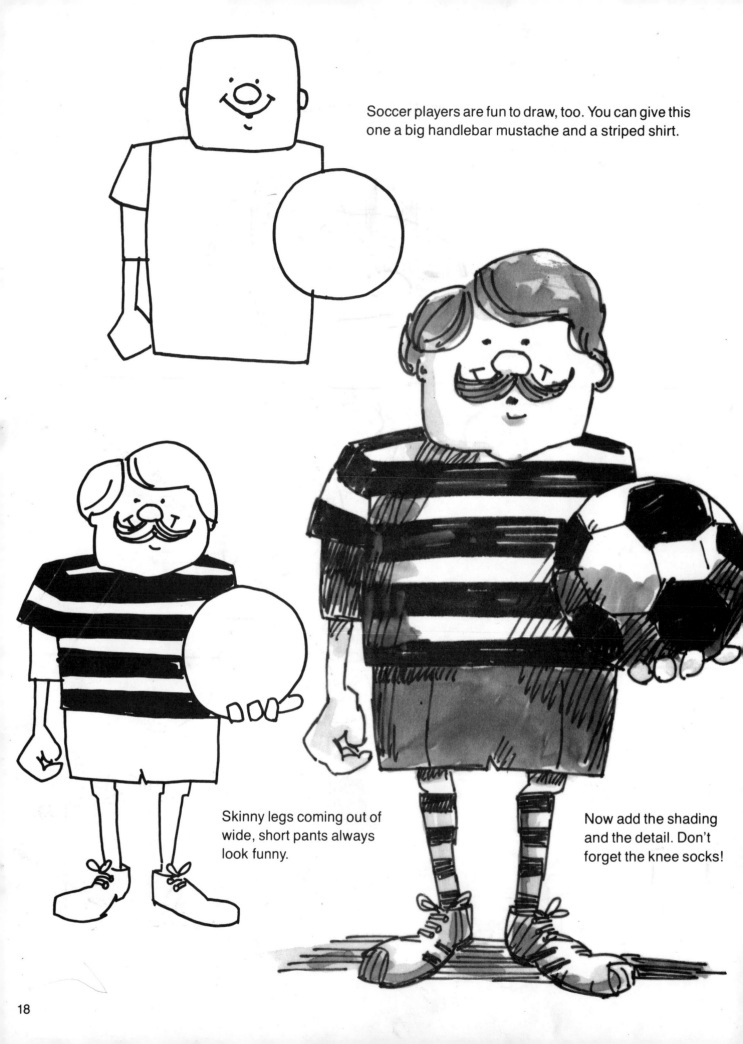

Soccer players are fun to draw, too. You can give this one a big handlebar mustache and a striped shirt.

Skinny legs coming out of wide, short pants always look funny.

Now add the shading and the detail. Don't forget the knee socks!

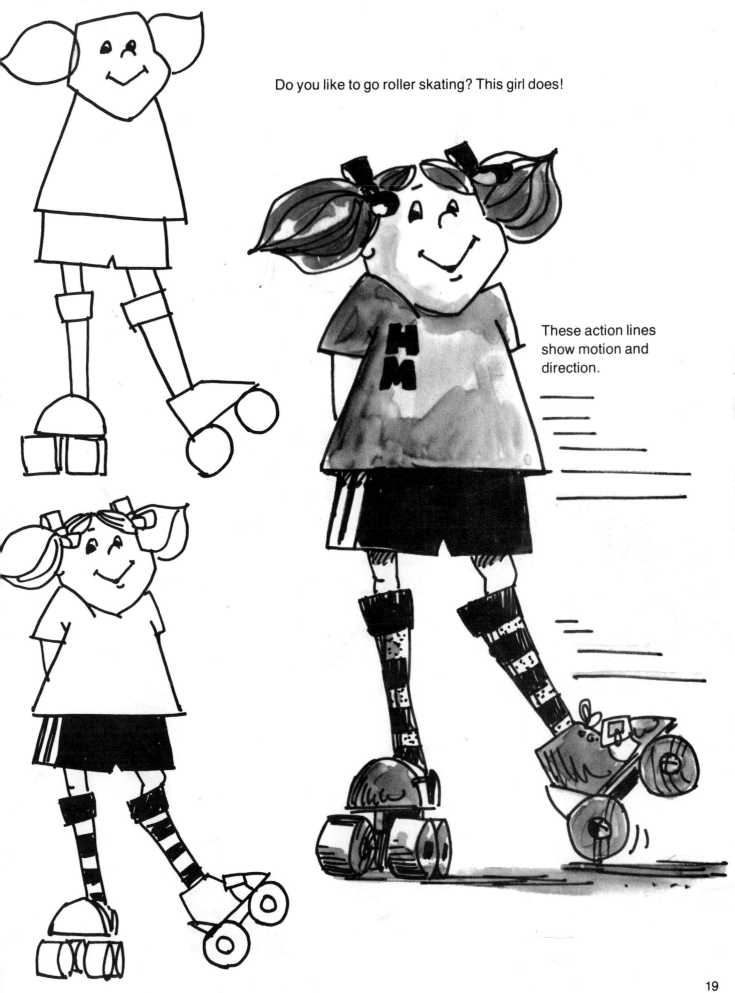

Do you like to go roller skating? This girl does!

These action lines show motion and direction.

19

Ever see a racing-car driver on a tricycle? If you draw a situation that is out of place or unexpected, it will usually look very funny.

Remember to start by using basic shapes to get the right proportions. Then join them and add the detail for the final drawing.

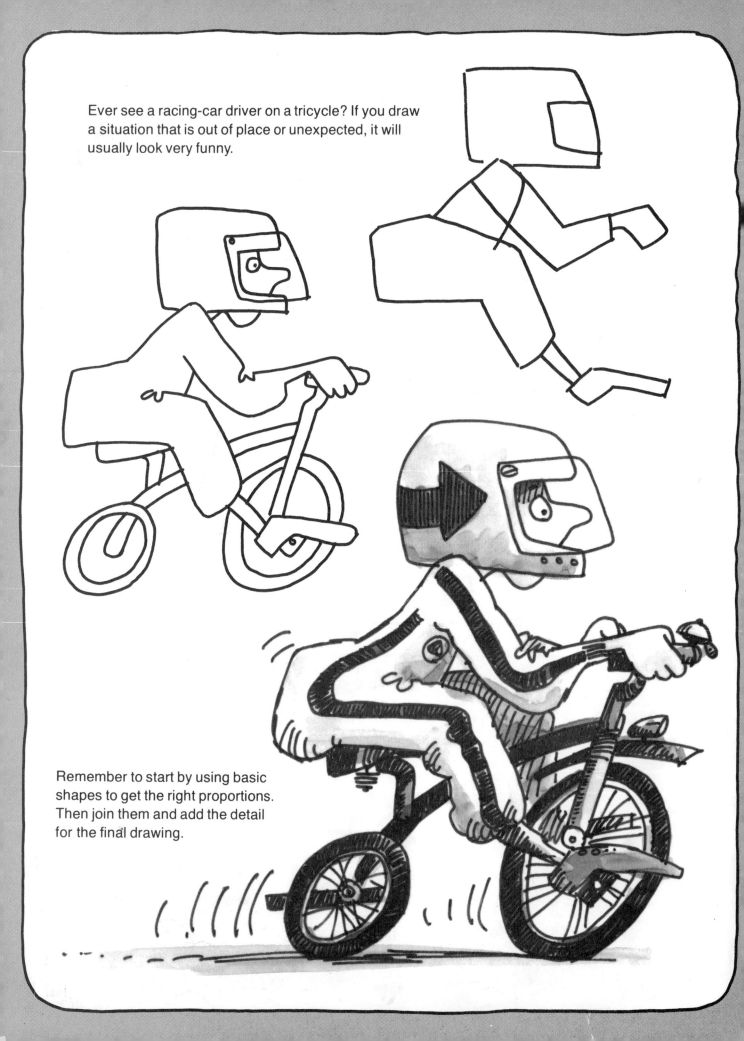

Now let's draw that driver with his race car.

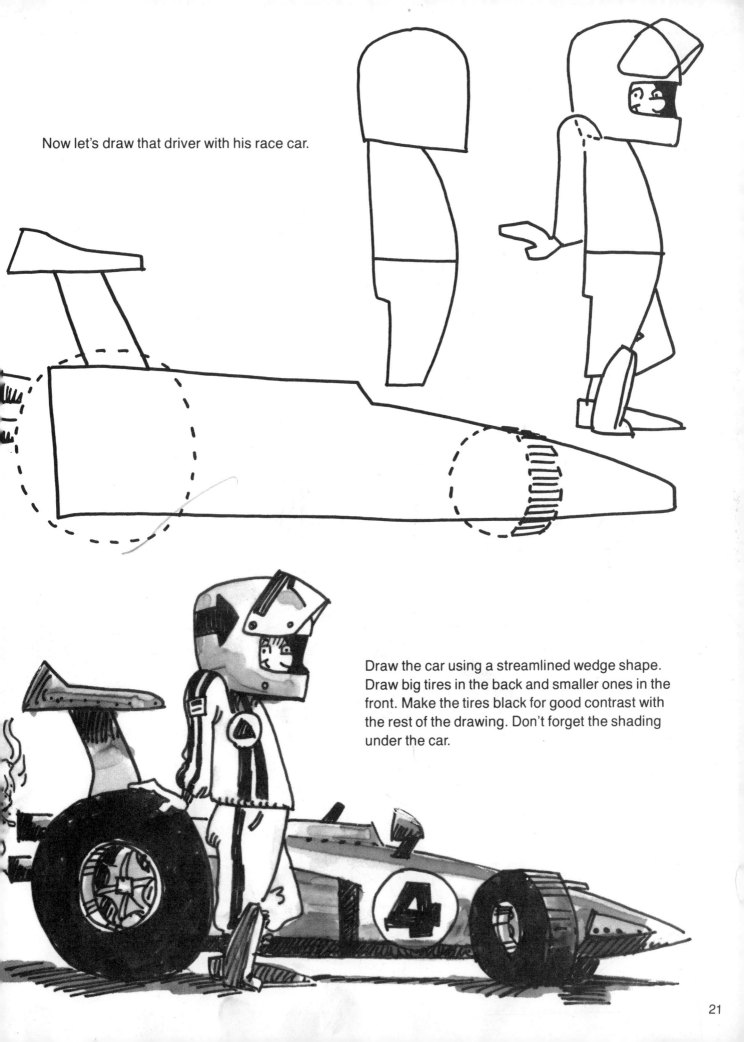

Draw the car using a streamlined wedge shape. Draw big tires in the back and smaller ones in the front. Make the tires black for good contrast with the rest of the drawing. Don't forget the shading under the car.

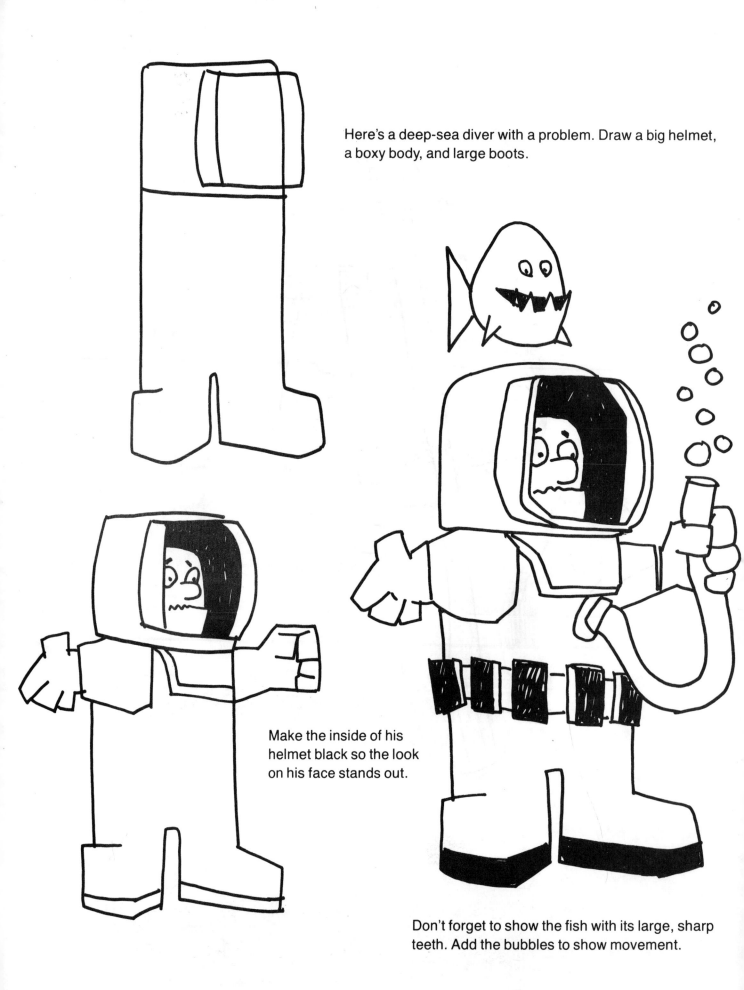

Here's a deep-sea diver with a problem. Draw a big helmet, a boxy body, and large boots.

Make the inside of his helmet black so the look on his face stands out.

Don't forget to show the fish with its large, sharp teeth. Add the bubbles to show movement.

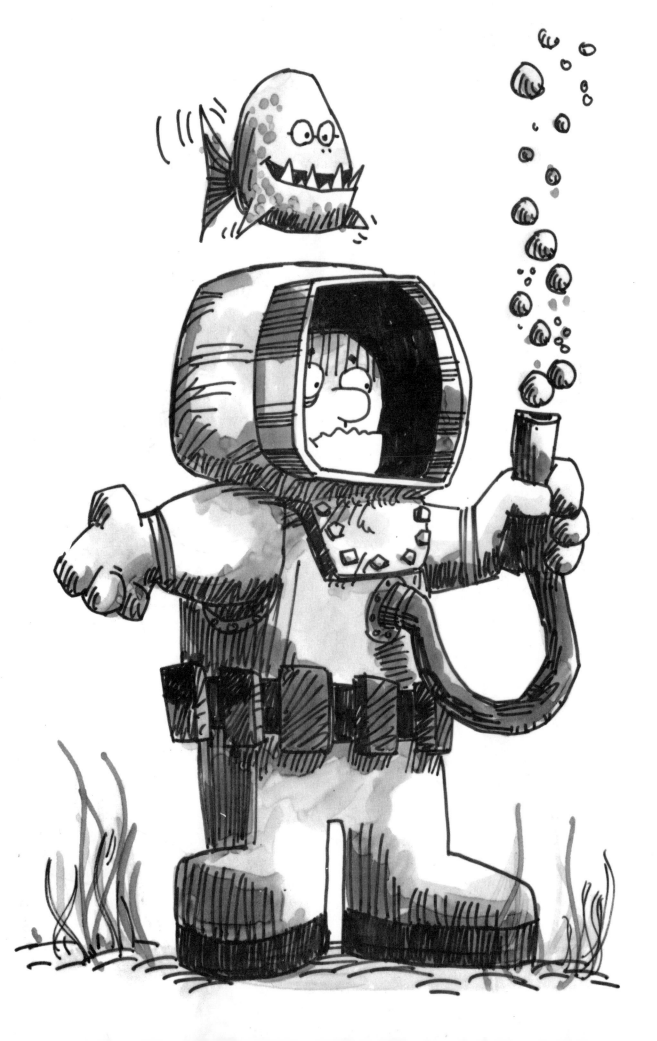

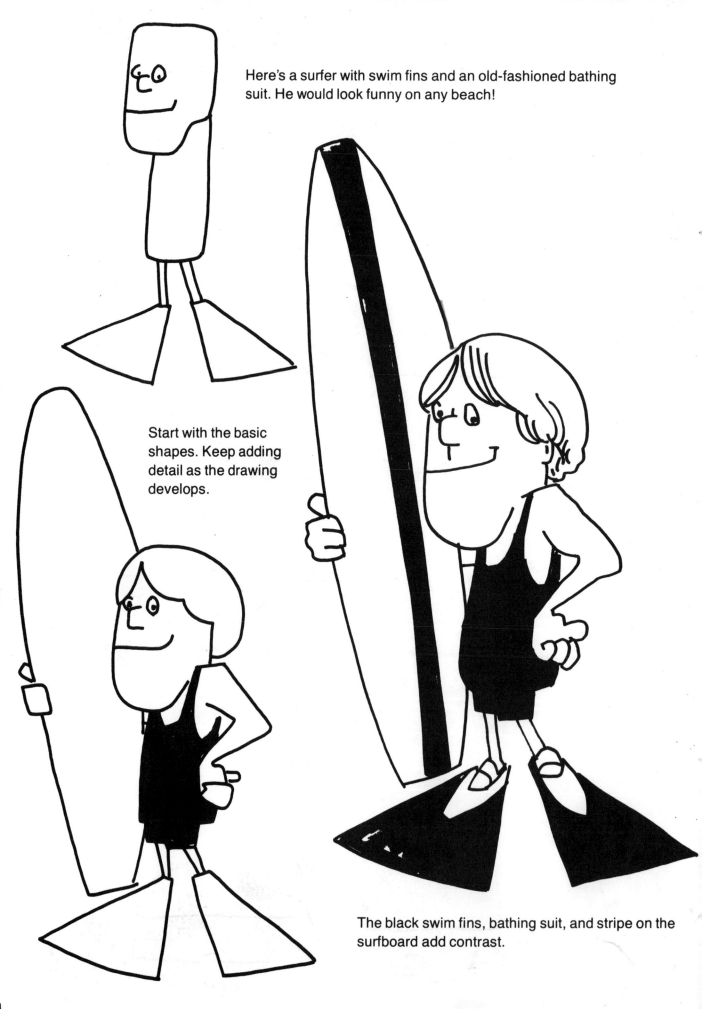

Here's a surfer with swim fins and an old-fashioned bathing suit. He would look funny on any beach!

Start with the basic shapes. Keep adding detail as the drawing develops.

The black swim fins, bathing suit, and stripe on the surfboard add contrast.

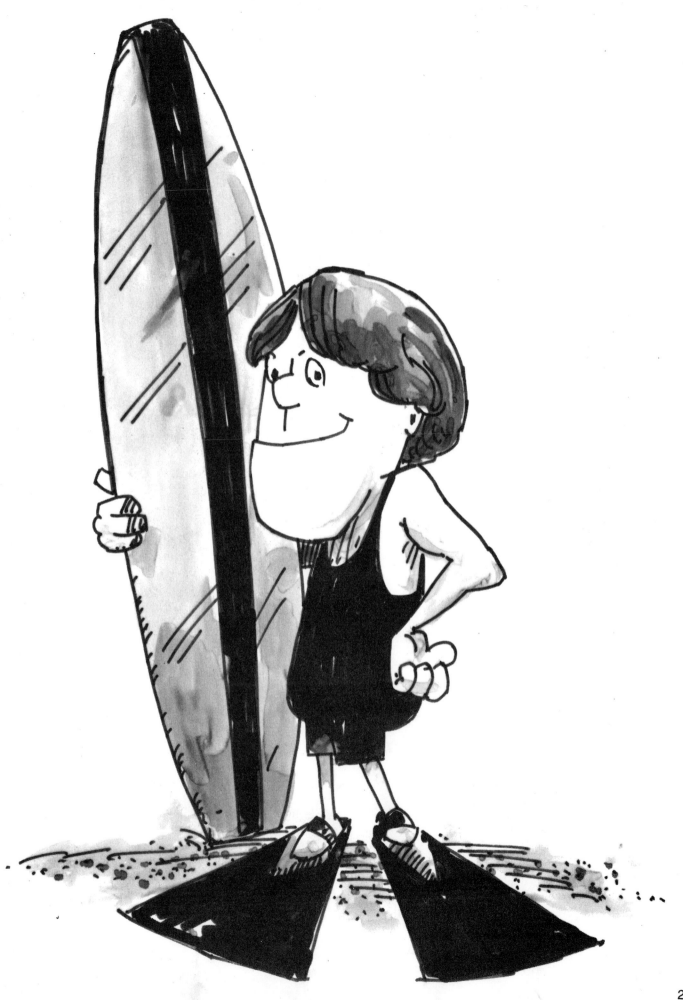

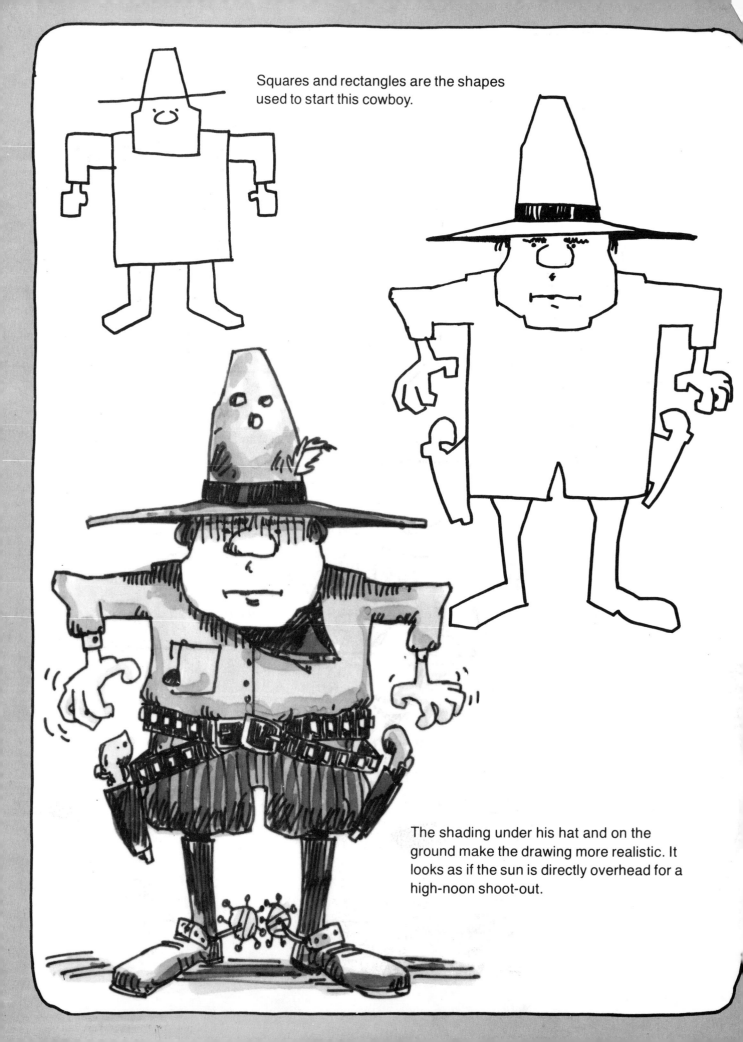

Squares and rectangles are the shapes used to start this cowboy.

The shading under his hat and on the ground make the drawing more realistic. It looks as if the sun is directly overhead for a high-noon shoot-out.

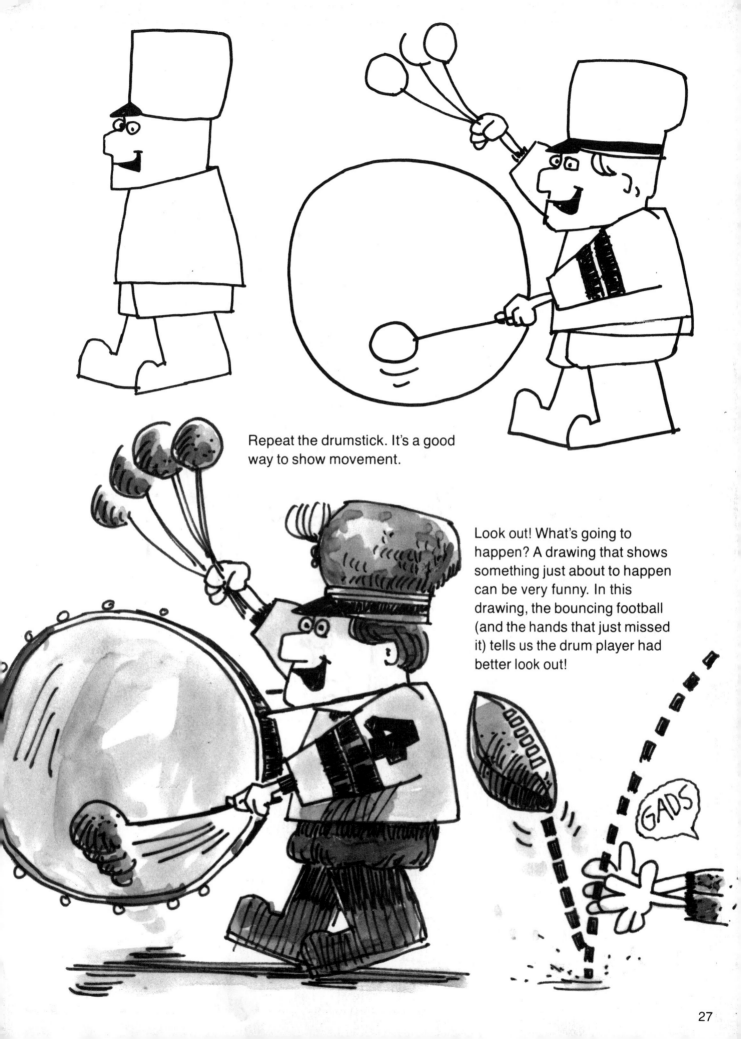

Repeat the drumstick. It's a good way to show movement.

Look out! What's going to happen? A drawing that shows something just about to happen can be very funny. In this drawing, the bouncing football (and the hands that just missed it) tells us the drum player had better look out!

GADS

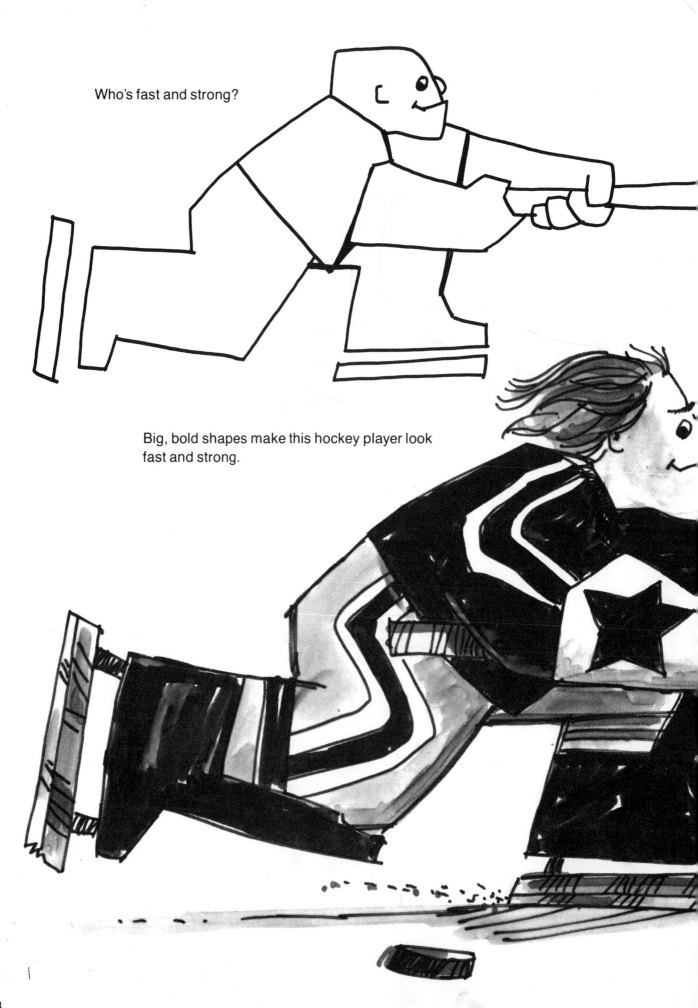

Who's fast and strong?

Big, bold shapes make this hockey player look
fast and strong.

28

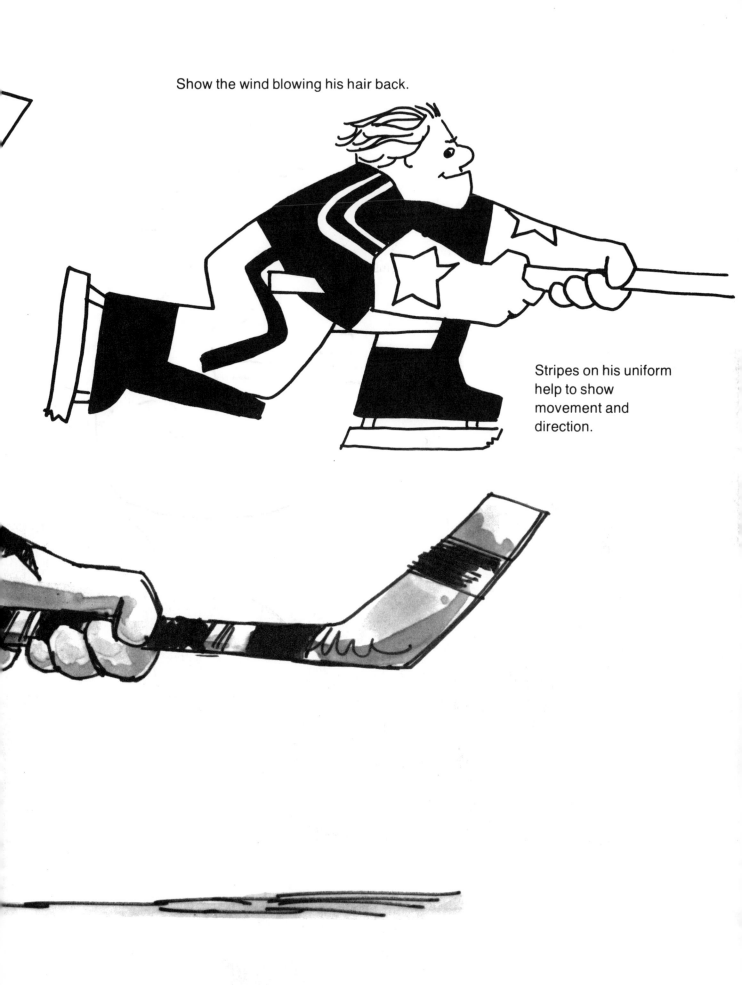

Show the wind blowing his hair back.

Stripes on his uniform help to show movement and direction.

Sometimes drawing a funny person starts with just a face.

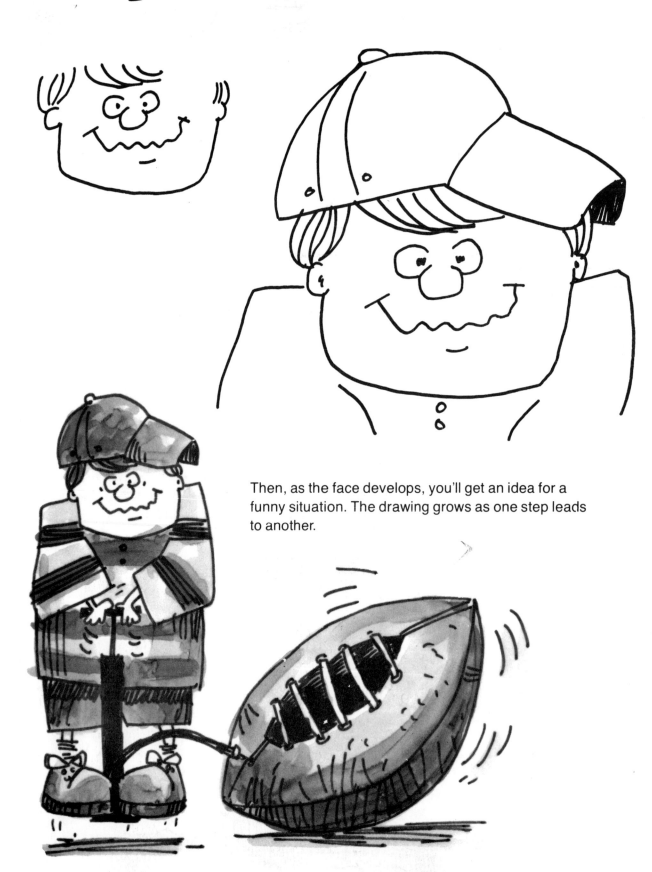

Then, as the face develops, you'll get an idea for a funny situation. The drawing grows as one step leads to another.

Buzz Bomber

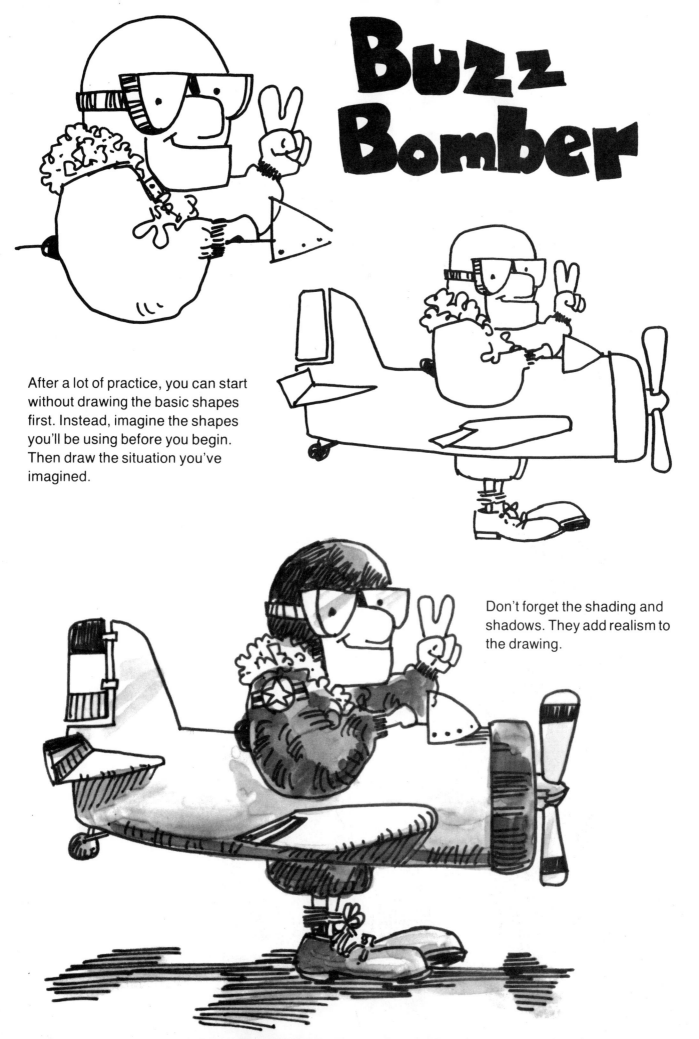

After a lot of practice, you can start without drawing the basic shapes first. Instead, imagine the shapes you'll be using before you begin. Then draw the situation you've imagined.

Don't forget the shading and shadows. They add realism to the drawing.

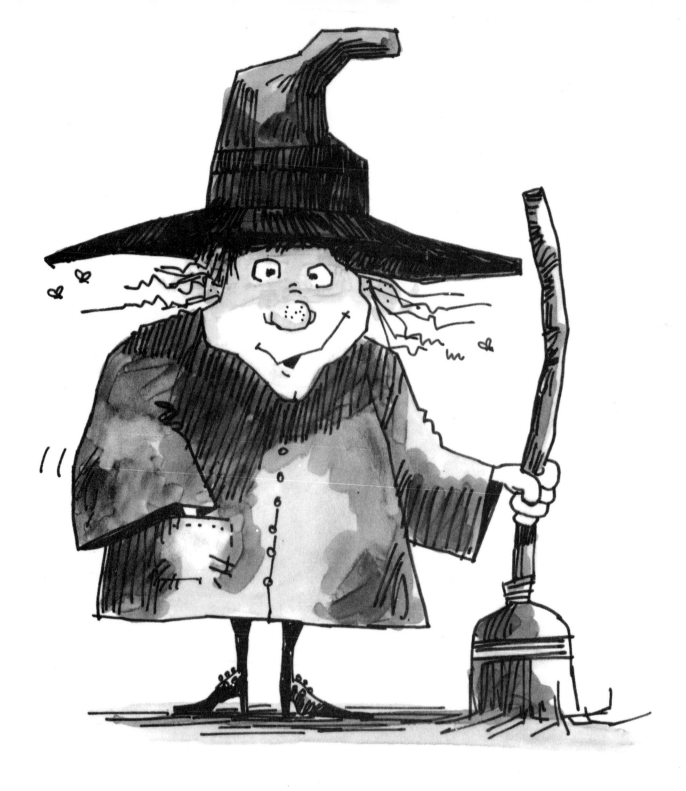

A little imagination and a sense of humor go a long way in the art of drawing funny people. As you practice, your own style and technique will grow. But remember, the most important thing of all is to have fun when you draw!